bl

BL stands for the Blue Blender! He puts letters together and makes the sounds of the letters glide together.

Help the Blue Blender make the words below. Add the right letters to make a word and answer the riddle. Then color the Blue Blender. Color his suit blue!

The color of the sky.   __ __ ue

You play with these.   __ __ ocks

The color of the night.   __ __ ack

You do this to birthday candles.   __ __ ow

cl

Cl stands for Clara Clown.
Color all the words that start with cl.

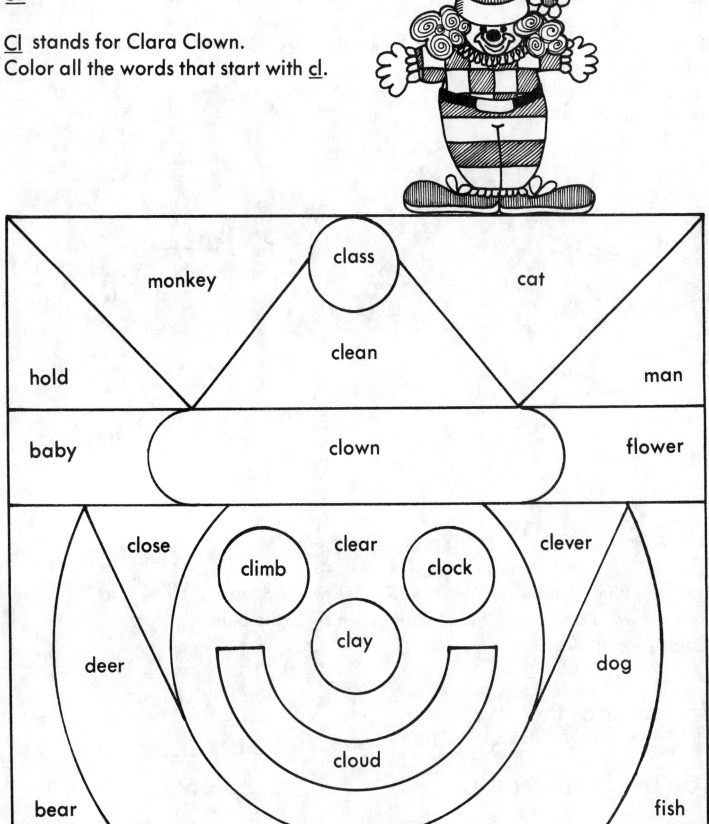

monkey

class

cat

clean

hold

man

baby

clown

flower

close

clear

clever

climb

clock

clay

deer

dog

cloud

bear

fish

The picture is of a _ _ _ _ _.

fl

<u>Fl</u> stands for Flora Flower.
Add <u>fl</u> to the words. Then draw a line from the word to the picture.

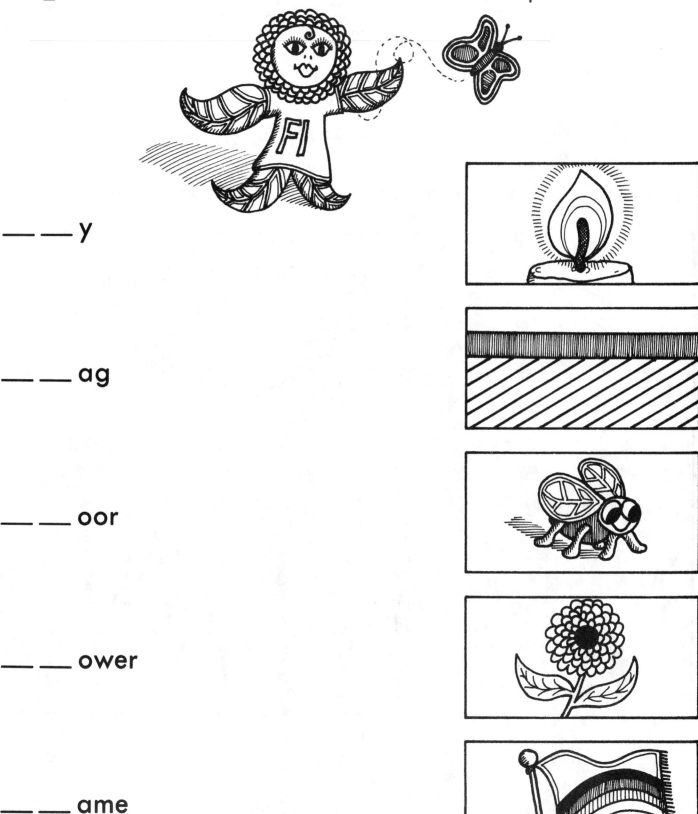

— — y

— — ag

— — oor

— — ower

— — ame

gl

Gl stands for Glad Gloria!

Wait! Glad Gloria is not glad! She is sad! She is sad because she has lost three things. They all begin with gl. Help her find the things. Draw a line around them. Then write the words below.

__ __ ove   __ __ ass   __ __ obe

How will Gloria feel when she finds the things she lost? __ __ __ __

pl

PI stands for please.

Circle the word that begins with pl.

1. pet   gold   plan

2. play   snake   blue

3. green   chair   plant

4. book   place   dark

5. please   clown   parade

Please place the plain platter on the platform for the school play.

sl

SI stands for Sleepy Slim.

Draw a line around the pictures that begin with the sl sound.

School Zone Publishing Co.

REVIEW: l blends

Are you handy with blends? Let's see if you are. Write each blend once to make a new word. Say the new word.

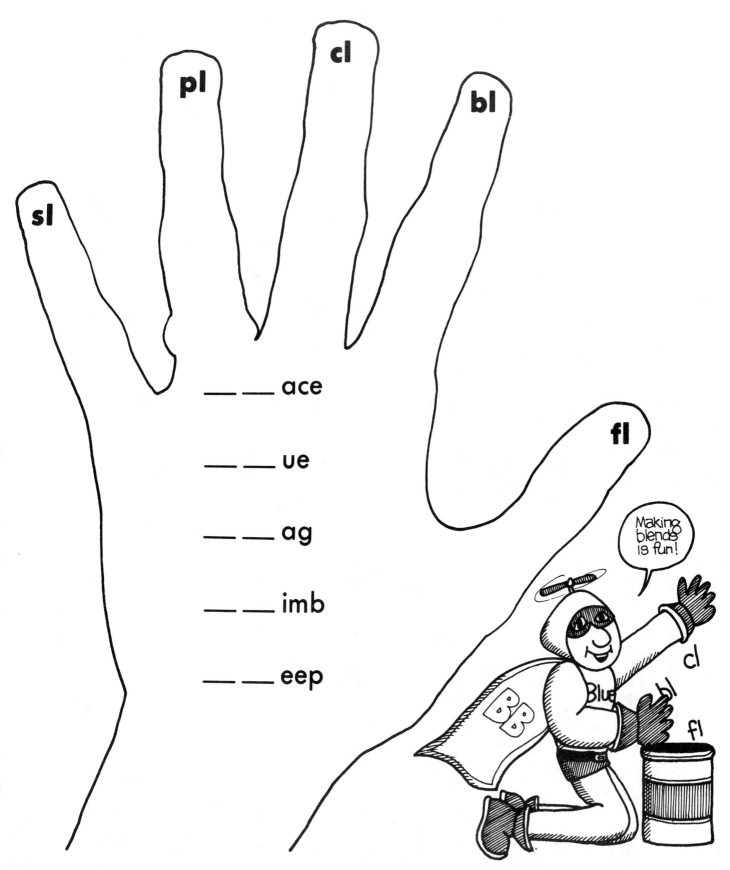

_ _ ace

_ _ ue

_ _ ag

_ _ imb

_ _ eep

Making blends is fun!

br

Br stands for branches.

Write the correct word on each branch. Say the word.

3. We had to go over a _____.

2. My _____ is six today.

1. I need a _____ and dust pan.

4. The sun was _____.

5. The man was _____.

6. The _____ fell from the tree.

branch

brave

bright

brook

broom

brother

My brother brags that he is brave.

School Zone Publishing Co.

cr

Cr stands for Crazy Crow.

Draw a line around six picture words that begin with cr.

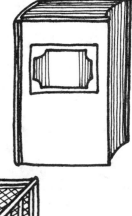

dr

Dr stands for drivers!

Color the dr words green.

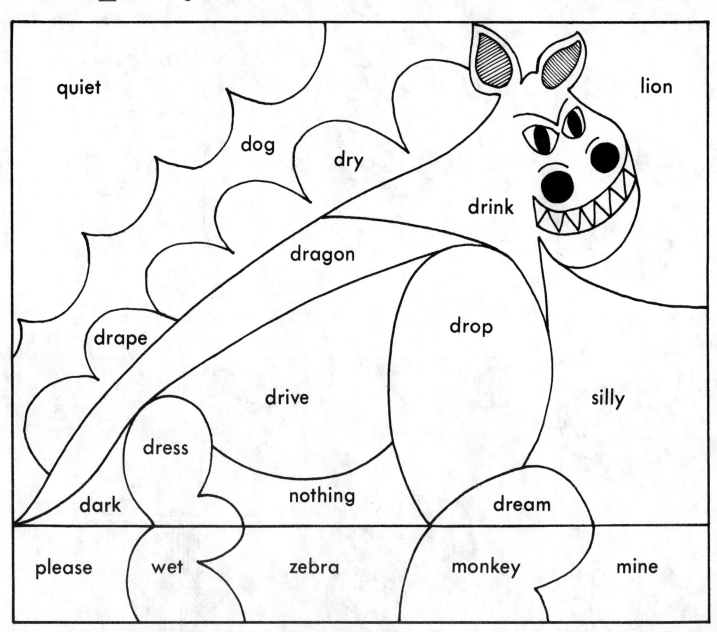

quiet

dog

dry

lion

drink

dragon

drape

drop

drive

silly

dress

dark

nothing

dream

please   wet   zebra   monkey   mine

This is a picture of a (dress dragon driver).

fr

Fr stands for Friendly Frog.

Friendly Frog likes to ask riddles. Read his riddles. Then write the answers.

frog	from	friend	front	fruits	frighten

1. Somebody you like is a _____.

2. It is not the back. It is the _____.

3. Suzie got a present _____ Jimmy.

4. A green animal that hops is a _____.

5. Apples, oranges, and bananas are _____.

6. If you scare somebody, you _____ them.

Here, Friendly Frog. Have some fresh fruit!

gr

Gr stands for green grass. Color the grass green.

Add gr to each word. Say the word.

1. __ __ een

2. __ __ ass

3. __ __ andmother

4. __ __ apes

5. __ __ asshopper

6. __ __ ill

7. __ __ andfather

School Zone Publishing Co.

pr

Pr stands for Proud Prince.

Connect the dots.
You will see what the Proud Prince is holding.

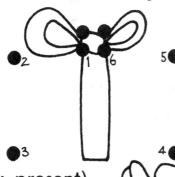

He is holding a (frog pretty present).

Draw a line around seven words that start with pr.

pretty

peanut

night

present

day

princess

prize

girl

pray

black

turtle

proud

prison

tr

Tr stands for train.

Draw a line around the blend that begins each picture word.

bl   pr
tr   pl

tr   br
gl   gr

cl   cr
bl   tr

tr   br
gr   pr

cl   tr
fr   br

fr   pl
pr   tr

Trudy tried a trick. She trapped a train.

School Zone Publishing Co.

REVIEW: r blends

Help the train go down the track. Make a word at each stop.
Use one of the blends to make a word.

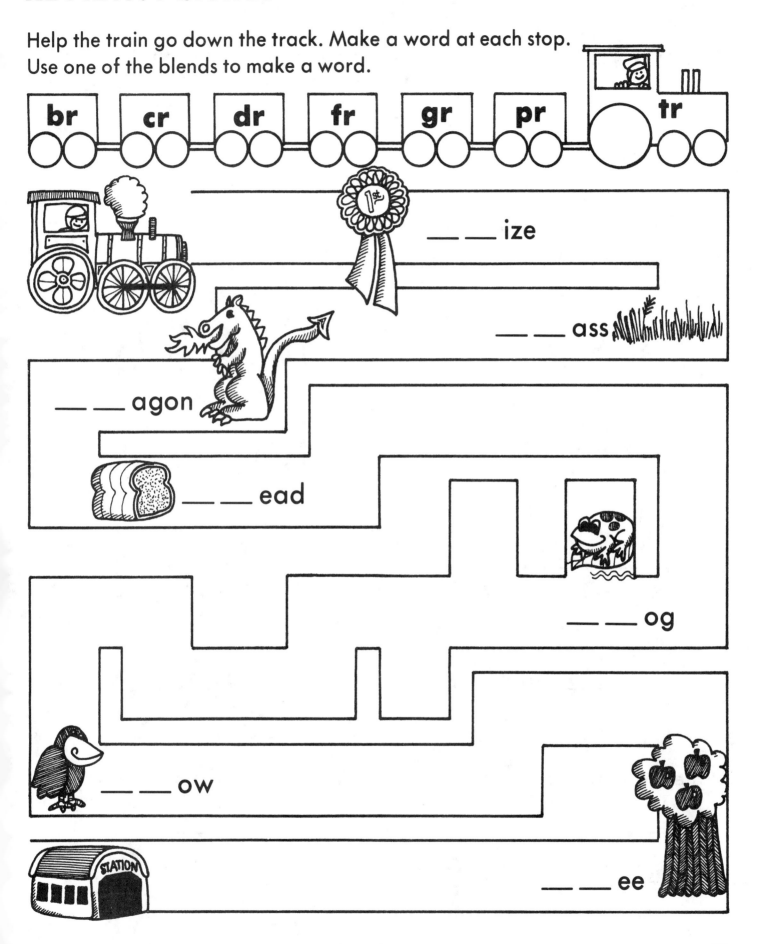

br   cr   dr   fr   gr   pr   tr

__ __ ize

__ __ ass

__ __ agon

__ __ ead

__ __ og

__ __ ow

__ __ ee

sw

Sw is for swim.

sp

Sp is for Spot.

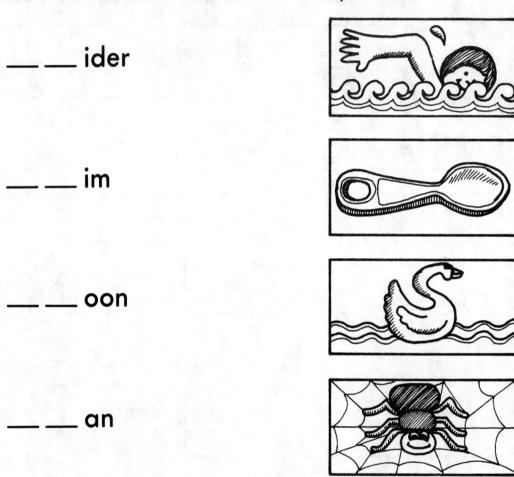

Make a word. Put the right letters in front of the word.
Say the word. Draw a line from the word to the picture.

__ __ ider

__ __ im

__ __ oon

__ __ an

Write two words that begin with sw.   Write two words that begin with sp.

_____   _____

_____   _____

    School Zone Publishing Co.

sm

Sm is for small.

sn

Sn is for snail.

Draw a line around the picture that starts with the blend in the box.

sm			
sn			
sn			
sm			
sm			
sn			

Smart snails always smile at snakes!

st

St is for Start and Stop!

Start and Stop are lost! Help them get home. Draw a line from Start and Stop to the next st word. Then to the next. If you follow the st words, Start and Stop will get home.

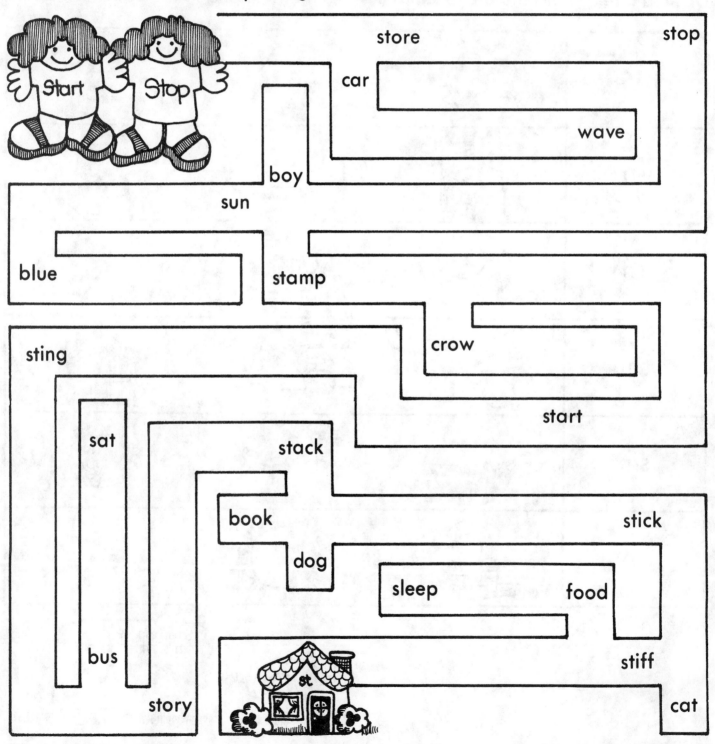

store   stop

car

wave

boy

sun

blue   stamp

crow

sting   start

sat   stack

book   stick

dog

sleep   food

bus   stiff

story   cat

st

St can also end words. Then it stands for last.
It is the last sound in last!

Color the words that end in st red.

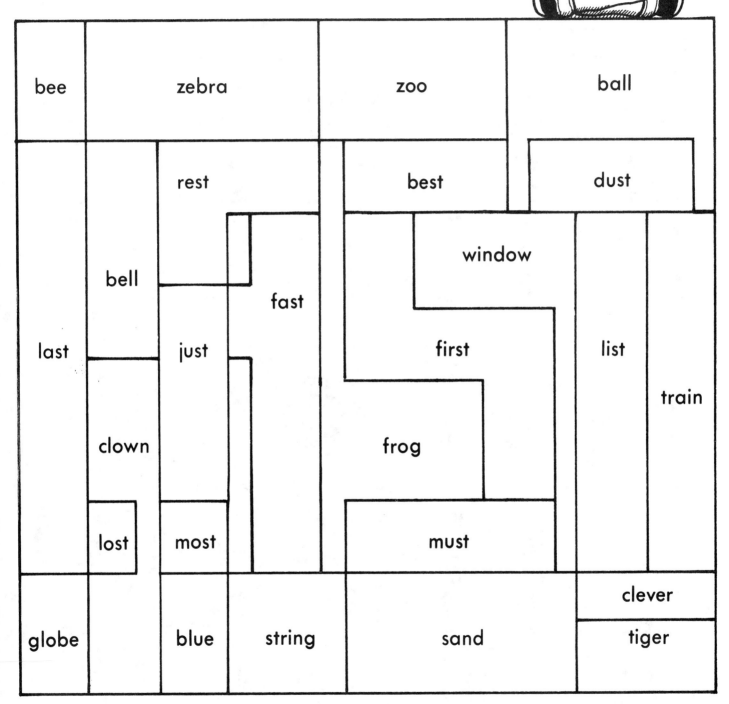

bee	zebra	zoo	ball
last	bell / rest / just / clown / lost	fast / best / window / first / frog / must / dust	list / train / clever / tiger
globe	blue	string	sand

The picture says ___ ___ ___ ___.

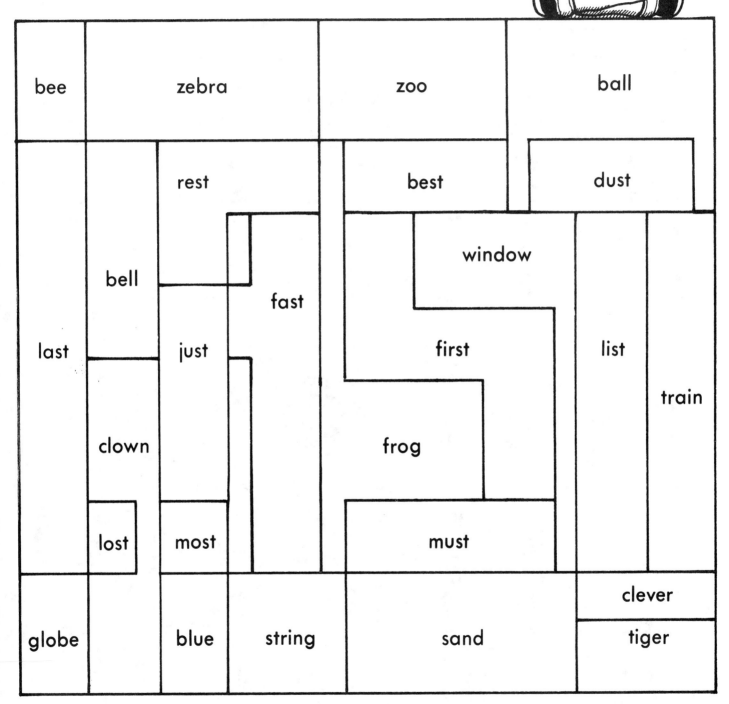

This is NOT the last page!

str

Str is for string.

spr

Spr is for spring.

Draw a line around the picture that starts with the blend given.

spr			
spr			
str			
str			
str			

REVIEW: s blends

Look at the picture. Say the picture word. Draw a line around the beginning blend. Write the blend on the blanks. Say the word.

str   **sl**

__ __ __ awberry

sl   **sn**

__ __ ail

sm   **st**

__ __ amp

sp   **str**

__ __ __ ing

st   **sw**

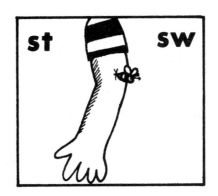

__ __ ing

st   **sm**

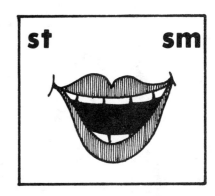

__ __ ile

sw   **sl**

__ __ im

sl   **st**

__ __ op

spr   **st**

__ __ __ ing

ch

Ch is for cheese.

Circle the picture that begins with the ch sound.

Ch is also for porch.

Circle the picture that ends with the ch sound.

School Zone Publishing Co.

sh

Sh is for sheep.   Sh is also for fish.

Sheep and Fish are all mixed up. They don't know which word belongs to them. Put all the words that start with <u>sh</u> in the sheep pen. Put all the words that end with <u>sh</u> in the fish pond.

ship	shell	dish	shoe	wish
show	shop	wash	shirt	push

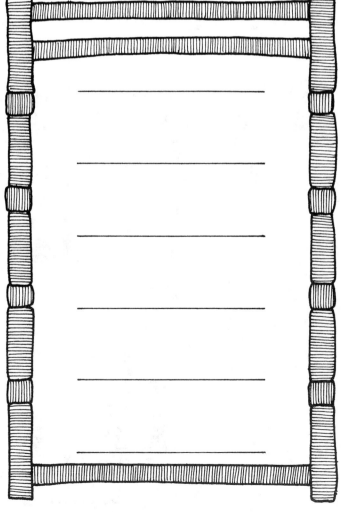 

th

<u>Th</u> is for thumb.

<u>Th</u> is also for mouth.

Here are some riddles. Put the correct word on the line to answer the riddle.

bath	south	thing	path	thank	think

1. "_____ you, Grandma," said Jeff.

2. Karen did not want to take a _____.

3. Birds fly _____ for the winter.

4. I _____ I know the answer.

5. What is this _____?

6. The _____ went into the woods.

School Zone Publishing Co.

wh

Wh is for whale.

Draw a line around the words or the pictures that begin with wh.

wh			
wh	wagon	vase	wheat
wh			
wh	man	woman	why
wh			
wh	green	white	yellow

DIGRAPH REVIEW: <u>ch</u>, <u>sh</u>, <u>th</u>, <u>wh</u>

Draw a line from the letters to the picture words that begin or end with them.

School Zone Publishing Co.

REVIEW

Match the socks to make words. Draw a line from each beginning sock to each ending sock.

1.

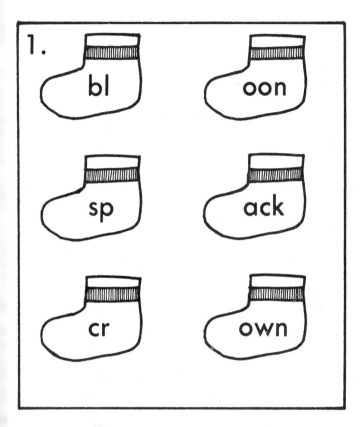

2.

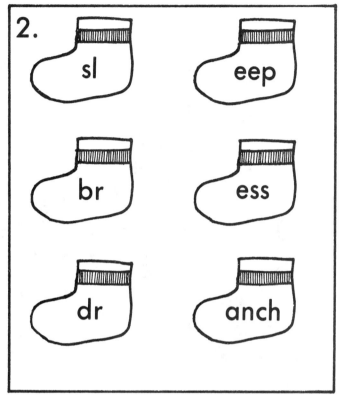

3.

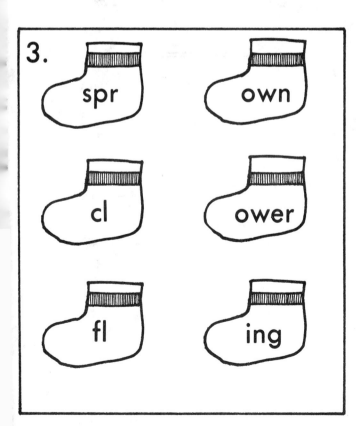

4.

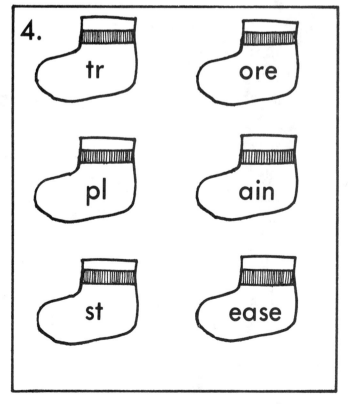

REVIEW

Help the Blue Blender. Make a word for each blend. Write it on the line.

_____   _____

_____   _____

_____   _____

_____   _____

_____   _____

DIGRAPHS REVIEW: <u>ch</u>, <u>sh</u>, <u>th</u>, <u>wh</u>

Draw a line from the letters to the picture words that begin with them.

REVIEW

Be a worker in the word factory! Make four words in each row. Add the right blend to the last three letters to make a word. Write each word on the line.

bl	br	cl	cr	dr	sl	sm	sn	st	tr

own   **ack**   **ick**

_____   _____   _____

_____   _____   _____

_____   _____   _____

_____   _____   _____

School Zone Publishing Co.